TOM BRADY

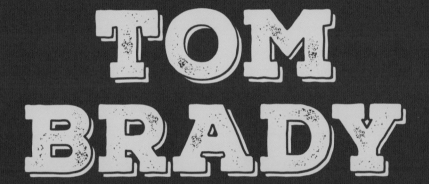

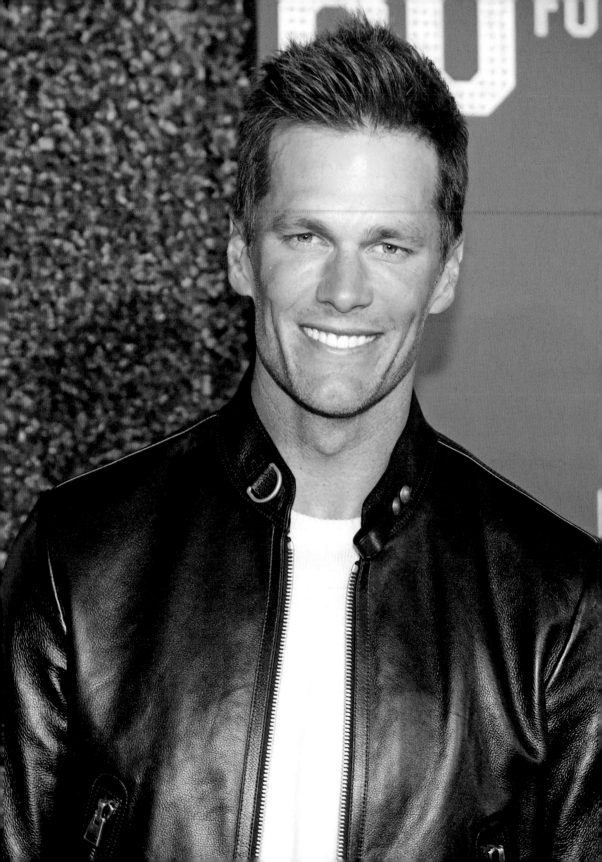

TOM BRADY

GRIDIRON G.O.A.T.

Leslie Holleran

LERNER PUBLICATIONS ◆ MINNEAPOLIS

For my family and friends, with heartfelt thanks for cheering me on

Lerner Publications Company
An imprint of Lerner Publishing Group, Inc.
241 First Avenue North
Minneapolis, MN 55401 USA

For reading levels and more information, look up this title at www.lernerbooks.com.

Main body text set in Rotis Serif Std 55 Regular. Typeface provided by Adobe Systems.

Designer: Lauren Cooper **Photo Editor:** Annie Zheng
Lerner team: Sue Marquis

Library of Congress Cataloging-in-Publication Data

Names: Holleran, Leslie, author.
Title: Tom Brady : gridiron G.O.A.T. / Leslie Holleran.
Other titles: Gridiron greatest of all time
Description: Minneapolis, MN : Lerner Publications, [2024] | Series: Gateway biographies ; 01
  | Includes bibliographical references and index. | Audience: Ages 9–14 years | Audience:
  Grades 4–6 | Summary: "With seven Super Bowl wins and five Super Bowl MVP awards, Tom
  Brady is the greatest quarterback of all time. Explore Brady's 23-year professional football
  career, his personal life, and what's next for the star"– Provided by publisher.
Identifiers: LCCN 2023018118 (print) | LCCN 2023018119 (ebook) | ISBN 9798765610428 (lib.
  bdg.) | ISBN 9798765623800 (pbk) | ISBN 9798765614624 (epub)
Subjects: LCSH: Brady, Tom, 1977-–Juvenile literature. | Quarterbacks (Football)–United
  States–Biography–Juvenile literature. | Football players–United States–Biography–Juvenile
  literature. | New England Patriots (Football team)–History–Juvenile literature. | Tampa Bay
  Buccaneers (Football team)–History–Juvenile literature. | Sportscasters–United States–
  Biography–Juvenile literature.
Classification: LCC GV939.B685 H65 2024 (print) | LCC GV939.B685 (ebook) | DDC
  796.332092 [B]–dc23/eng/20230518

LC record available at https://lccn.loc.gov/2023018118
LC ebook record available at https://lccn.loc.gov/2023018119

Manufactured in the United States of America
1-1009627-51715-8/15/2023

TABLE OF CONTENTS

New England Patriots quarterback Tom Brady completed 43 passes in the 2017 Super Bowl. He broke the all-time Super Bowl record of 37 completions that he had set two years earlier.

In 2017 Tom Brady, one of the best quarterbacks in the National Football League (NFL), led his team to the Super Bowl for the seventh time. No other player had ever been to more than six Super Bowls. Brady and the New England Patriots faced the Atlanta Falcons at NRG Stadium in Houston, Texas, on February 5. New England was hoping for another Super Bowl win—their fifth since Brady took over as quarterback 15 years earlier. Since joining the team, he had gone from playing backup quarterback to becoming an NFL superstar. Many of Brady's family members were in the stands to cheer him on, including his mother, who had recently finished treatment for cancer.

Devonta Freeman soars into the end zone for Atlanta's first touchdown.

In the second quarter, the Falcons scored three touchdowns in less than 10 minutes of game time and led 21–3 at halftime. Falcons players were dancing in the locker room, confident that victory would be theirs. Meanwhile, in the Patriots locker room, coaches encouraged their team to keep fighting.

The Falcons' lead grew to 28–3 in the third quarter. Most fans and football experts believed Atlanta's victory was certain. Some New England fans left the game early, but they missed a remarkable comeback by the Patriots. Brady led his team down the field 75 yards for a touchdown. The drive included a 15-yard run by Brady— the longest rushing play of the day. The score was 28–9 at the start of the fourth quarter.

A field goal by the Patriots brought the score to 28–12 with 10 minutes left. A Falcons fumble gave the ball back to the Patriots for their next scoring opportunity. Brady threw a six-yard touchdown pass to receiver Danny Amendola. Running back James White then took a direct snap for a two-point conversion to make the score 28–20.

With just over three minutes to go in the fourth quarter, Brady led another drive down the field. He threw a pass that was nearly intercepted by a Falcons defender. Instead, Patriots wide receiver Julian Edelman made a remarkable diving catch as the ball bounced off the defender's shoe.

After three more completions, Brady passed the ball to White, who ran in for a one-yard touchdown. Brady then completed a two-point conversion pass to Amendola. The score was tied at 28. For the first time ever, the Super Bowl was going into overtime. In the locker room before overtime began, Edelman encouraged his quarterback. "Let's win this thing," Edelman said to Brady. "For your mom."

The Patriots received the ball first in overtime. They never let the Falcons touch it again. New England scored a touchdown and won 34–28, completing the biggest comeback in Super Bowl history.

Brady has always performed his best when the game is on the line. This time, the victory was dedicated to one of the most important people in his life—his mother. Brady's football dreams turned out better than he ever imagined, but they didn't come easily.

PLAYING TO WIN

Thomas Edward Patrick Brady Jr. was born on August 3, 1977, in San Mateo, California. He was the fourth child of Galynn and Thomas Brady. He has three older sisters: Maureen, Julie, and Nancy.

The Bradys enjoyed playing sports and going to games as fans. They had season tickets to San Francisco 49ers football games. Four-year-old Tom was at the 1981 National Football Conference Championship

Brady holds the Vince Lombardi Trophy in victory for the fifth time after helping the Patriots beat the Falcons in 2017.

Joe Montana won four Super Bowls with the San Francisco 49ers between 1982 and 1990.

game when 49ers quarterback Joe Montana led his team to a thrilling victory. It was an exciting time to be a 49ers fan, and Montana became one of Tom's favorite players.

The Bradys' neighborhood was full of kids. They played games of kickball, basketball, baseball, soccer, and touch football. All four Brady kids joined in. Tom's parents wouldn't let him play tackle football until high school, so he played other sports instead. He started Little League baseball at eight years old. He practiced hitting, throwing, and catching with his dad at a park. Tom and his father also had a Sunday ritual: playing golf together.

Brady with his parents at an awards show in 2005

Tom loved the neighborhood games, but he was picked on by older kids and had difficulty keeping up. What Tom lacked in ability, he made up for in spirit. Even losing a video game made him mad. Tom once challenged another kid to a race and lost, but Tom kept challenging him until he won. He refused to give up, a trait that helped him when he began playing football in high school. Though he had a strong, accurate arm, he didn't know how to play quarterback.

DRIVEN TO SUCCEED

Tom went to Junipero Serra High School in San Mateo, an all-boys Catholic school a short distance from his home. Baseball was his best sport, but he dreamed of becoming a great football player like Montana. So Tom tried out for the freshman football team.

Tom quickly realized how far he had to go to realize his dreams. He didn't get to play quarterback during his first season with the freshman team. He played linebacker and tight end, but he wasn't especially good at either position, and the team lost every game.

Tom was determined to get better. In the summer, he spent time at a football camp at the College of San Mateo. Tom's prospects for playing time improved tremendously in his sophomore year. The junior varsity starting quarterback quit the team to focus on basketball, and Tom took his place. As the starter, Tom helped the football team achieve a 5–4 record.

Despite improving, he wasn't a shoo-in for the varsity football team the next year. Serra's varsity head coach, Tom MacKenzie, told him that he needed to work on throwing and getting stronger. He took the coach's advice and began working with a personal trainer. MacKenzie said, "I don't think I ever had to tell him to work hard again. Because he didn't start out as a superstar, he learned how important it was to keep learning and growing as an athlete."

In the summer after his sophomore year, Tom did a three-hour workout every day. He didn't even stop during

The Junipero Serra High School football field

his family's summer vacation. The effort paid off, and he became the varsity team's starting quarterback his junior year. During the season, he kept the pressure on himself both as an athlete and a student. The team had a winning 6–4 season, and he did well in school.

Tom began working on his college plans in the spring of his junior year. He wanted to go to a school with a good football team, and his father helped him by sending a videotape of his best plays to over 50 college programs. On the tape, MacKenzie introduced Tom and gave him a positive endorsement, noting his strong work ethic. It also showed Tom making different kinds of throws, such as deep passes down the sideline and quick, short passes in the middle of the field. The tape generated interest from the University of Michigan; the University of California, Berkeley; and other schools. Tom and his dad visited football camps at some of the schools during the summer.

Tom led the Serra football team to a mediocre 5–5 record his senior season, but he still drew interest from dozens of colleges. A recruiting visit to Michigan helped him choose the school. He said, "I loved the social aspect. I loved the team. It was a great school. It was more of a feeling. Once I experienced that, I really didn't want to go anywhere else."

Two-Sport Talent

Tom played catcher for Serra's varsity baseball team and excelled at defense. He was so good that the Seattle Mariners invited him to an open tryout in Seattle, Washington, in 1995. The Mariners and other Major League Baseball teams thought Brady had the skills to succeed at the sport's highest level, and the Montreal Expos drafted him in 1995. But Brady had his sights set on a football career.

In the spring of 1995, Tom shared with his family that he was going to Michigan. His dad had wanted him to choose California, Berkeley, where he would be close to home, but Tom had his heart set on Michigan. A few days later, Michigan's head football coach personally delivered a letter of intent to Tom. He signed it and officially committed to the school and its team. After graduation, he headed east to play football with the Michigan Wolverines.

Fans cheer for the Wolverines at Michigan Stadium. The stadium's nickname is the Big House because it can hold more than 107,000 people during games.

COLLEGE CHAMPION

Brady's college football career at Michigan got off to a rough start. At his first practice, he learned that he was at the bottom of the quarterback depth chart behind several others. Then the team's new head coach, Lloyd Carr, redshirted him. Redshirted players can practice with the team but don't play in games. A redshirt year doesn't count against an athlete's eligibility, so Brady was still eligible to play four seasons of college football.

Brady had few opportunities to show fans his passing skills during his first two years at Michigan.

The following year, Brady's situation didn't change much. He was no longer redshirted, but he played in only two games. The first pass he threw as a college quarterback was intercepted by a UCLA linebacker who returned it for a touchdown.

Brady considered transferring to a different school for more playing opportunities. He discussed his concerns with his coach, and Carr told him to focus on what he could do to improve. Brady chose not

Lloyd Carr won 122 games as head coach of the Wolverines from 1995 to 2007.

to leave Michigan. He told his coach, "I'm going to prove to you that I'm a great quarterback." According to Carr, Brady became fully committed to the team. He worked harder than ever and trained with Assistant Athletic Director Greg Harden to become mentally tougher.

For the 1997 season, Brady was the backup to starting quarterback Brian Griese. The Wolverines had an undefeated season, including a five-point Rose Bowl victory against Washington State. Brady learned a lot from the experience, and the next year he was ready to be Michigan's starting quarterback. Griese had joined the NFL, but athletic prodigy Drew Henson presented new competition for the Michigan job. To make matters worse for Brady, most Wolverines fans wanted Henson, a talented freshman from Brighton, Michigan, to start. Fans cheered for Henson when he came onto the field, and they booed Brady. He was going to have to prove himself, not only to his coach and teammates but also to Michigan fans.

Brady hands the ball to a running back during a 1998 victory against Michigan State.

The boos soon turned to cheers. Henson played in seven games in 1998, but Brady was the team's main quarterback. After losing the first two games, Brady led the Wolverines to victory in 10 of their final 11 matchups. One of those wins was a come-from-behind triumph over Arkansas in the Citrus Bowl.

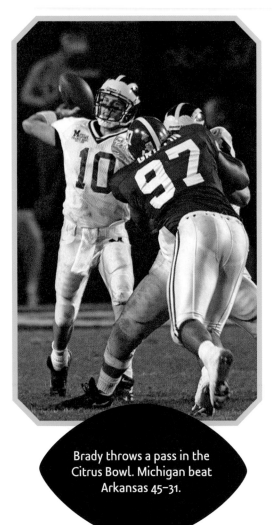

Brady throws a pass in the Citrus Bowl. Michigan beat Arkansas 45–31.

In Brady's final season at Michigan, Coach Carr continued rotating the quarterback position. Brady would start, and Henson would play the second quarter. At halftime, Carr would decide who would finish the game. Brady played the second half in four of the first five games, and Michigan won all five. Then Carr changed the quarterback rotation, and they lost two games. Finally, Carr decided Brady would start the remainder of the 1999 season.

Brady never lost another college football game. His ultimate triumph was leading Michigan to a thrilling 35–34 victory over Alabama in the Orange Bowl on New Year's Day in 2000. He completed 34 passes for 369 yards and four touchdowns. His college football career ended with a win and a great personal performance. Carr said, "He made believers out of everybody here. He represents everything that's positive about being an athlete." As for Brady, he was ready to take his game to the next level—the NFL.

JOINING THE BIG LEAGUE

When the 2000 NFL Draft took place in mid-April, Brady was a long shot. He had performed poorly at the NFL combine, the showcase where players eligible for the draft show off their speed, strength, and football skills. Brady ran the 40-yard dash in 5.28 seconds. Faster players ran it in under 5 seconds. His vertical jump was 24.5 inches (62.2 cm), the worst result for a quarterback that year. His poor combine performance led to a scouting report full of negative comments. In addition, NFL coaches were puzzled by his college record. They wondered why he had to share the quarterback position with Drew Henson when most NFL quarterbacks had been college starters, not part-time players.

Brady was far from being a great prospect, but he had come to the attention of Dick Rehbein, the New England Patriots quarterbacks coach. He had seen Brady play during Michigan's Pro Day, when pro scouts visited the school and evaluated the team's players. Rehbein believed that Brady had NFL potential. Coach Carr gave Brady a strong recommendation, and Chris Floyd, Brady's former Michigan teammate and a fullback with the Patriots, did as well. Floyd said, "If I had a question about a play and didn't want to go to a coach, I went to Tom because I knew he would always have the answer."

Brady spent the draft at home with his family, gathered around the TV to watch. The first day passed, and Brady wasn't picked. On the second day of the draft, the third, fourth, and fifth rounds took place, but no team chose Brady. He was disappointed and stopped watching the TV coverage, but Rehbein and Patriots head coach Bill Belichick were ready to make a move. They selected Brady in the sixth round with the 199th overall pick. Brady's hard work had finally paid off, and his dream to play in the NFL was coming true.

Like his first season of college football,

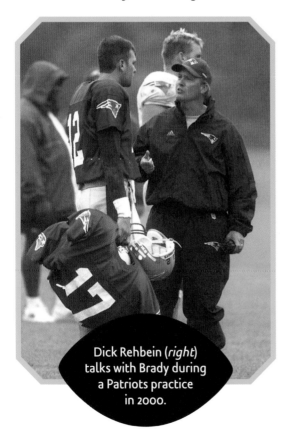

Dick Rehbein (*right*) talks with Brady during a Patriots practice in 2000.

In 2000 Tom Brady (*right*) wasn't a threat to Drew Bledsoe (*left*), but Brady would soon take Bledsoe's job.

Brady began his NFL career on the bench. He was one of three backup quarterbacks to starter Drew Bledsoe. Brady played in only one game that season, but he was determined to succeed in the NFL. Brady said, "My offseason my first year wasn't spent going on vacation. It was [in Massachusetts], working out and watching film and trying to get better." He returned for his second season with improved speed, mobility, and confidence.

WINNING MACHINE

Before the 2001 season opener, Brady became Bledsoe's first backup. Brady had played well in four preseason games and earned the promotion. When Bledsoe was injured in the second game of the season, Brady got his opportunity. He came off the bench and played the final minutes of a 10–3 New York Jets victory.

During the two months Bledsoe missed, Brady filled in and performed well, helping the Patriots win five of eight games. When Bledsoe returned in November, Belichick decided that Brady would continue to be the team's starter. Many fans were surprised, especially because Bledsoe had signed a $103 million contract, the NFL's richest contract at the time, earlier that year. But Brady was ready and had demonstrated his ability to lead the team.

During games, Brady could scan the opposing defense, predict how the play would unfold, and find an open wide receiver. Belichick said, "I'll get mad at him and say, 'Why did you do that?' And he'll say, 'Well, I saw the corner here, I saw the linebacker there. It looked like the receiver slipped a bit on his cut . . . .'"

Later, Belichick would look at video of the play and see that Brady had described exactly what happened. Even Bledsoe, who had to watch Brady take over as quarterback, praised the young passer. Bledsoe said, "It's not an accident that he has come in and played very, very well. He has worked at it, and honestly has earned everything he has done this year."

Brady led the Patriots throughout the remaining 2001 season. The team finished with an 11–5 record, a major turnaround from the previous year's losing season. In January 2002, the team clinched the American Football Conference (AFC) title, beating the Pittsburgh Steelers 24–17. The Patriots were going to meet the St. Louis Rams, whose offense was nicknamed the Greatest Show on Turf, in the Super Bowl.

Going into the game, the Patriots were 14-point underdogs. Brady told himself it was just another game, but it was the biggest moment of his career to date. The Super Bowl is the most popular sports event in the US, and more than 86 million people watched the game on TV.

With the score tied at 17 in the fourth quarter and less than 90 seconds remaining on the game clock, the Patriots needed to score. Brady led the team to the 30-yard line and spiked the ball to stop the clock. The New England placekicker, Adam Vinatieri, came on and kicked the

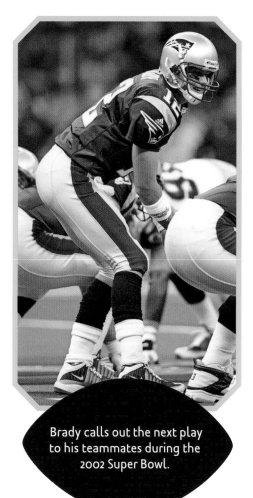

Brady calls out the next play to his teammates during the 2002 Super Bowl.

Adam Vinatieri (*second from right*) kicks a 48-yard field goal to win the 2002 Super Bowl for the Patriots.

winning field goal as time expired. New England's 20–17 victory was the first time in Super Bowl history that a team won the game on the final play. The Patriots had their first NFL championship, and Brady set a record as the youngest quarterback to win the big game.

The victory brought sudden fame to Brady, but he was determined to stay focused on his goals. "There are so many distractions that can make you lose sight of what's important," Brady said. He wasn't going to let that happen to him. "I know how I got here, and I'm going to devote myself to helping my team win it all again."

Brady meant what he said. With their superstar quarterback leading the way, the Patriots won the Super Bowl again in 2004 and 2005. They became one of only seven teams to win back-to-back Super Bowls. Brady and Belichick had created a Patriots dynasty, and they were determined to keep winning.

Brady (center) celebrates New England's 32–29 victory against the Carolina Panthers in the 2004 Super Bowl. His three touchdown passes helped him earn the Super Bowl MVP award for the second time.

GAME CHANGER

Brady had become the NFL's biggest star, and his popularity stretched beyond the football field. In April 2005, he hosted the late-night comedy show *Saturday Night Live.* His football accomplishments also created a lot of interest in his personal life. Brady was a famous young bachelor, and his romantic life became a hot topic with fans. A *60 Minutes* interviewer asked if he was considering marriage, but Brady wasn't dishing out many details on national TV. He said that his then girlfriend, model and actress Bridget Moynahan, was one of his best friends. He mostly kept the interview focused on his first love: football.

Bridget Moynahan and Brady

Brady dated Moynahan from early 2004 to late 2006. Their son, John "Jack" Moynahan, arrived in August 2007. Meanwhile, the Patriots were preparing for their next season. It had already been a momentous year for Brady with the birth of his first child, and it would prove to be a historic football season as well.

Before the 2007 season, the Patriots acquired two star players to beef up the team's receiving corps: Wes Welker and Randy Moss. Welker was an expert at catching short, quick passes, while Moss had game-breaking speed and talent. The Patriots were out to dominate, and they succeeded. They scored more touchdowns than any team in NFL history at the time. The Patriots won several games by as few as three points, but they didn't lose a game all season. Brady passed for 50 touchdowns, breaking Peyton Manning's 2004 NFL record of 49. Brady also set a new record for passing yards in a season with 4,806.

After winning 16 straight regular season games, New England won two playoff games to reach the Super Bowl. The stakes were even higher this time—they wanted a perfect season. But the New York Giants, led by quarterback Eli Manning, won the game 17–14. Their defense was fierce, and they managed to sack Brady five times. He said, "We usually are on the better side of those three-point wins."

Any hope of quickly returning to the Super Bowl was foiled during the 2008 season opener against the Kansas City Chiefs. A hit to Brady's left knee resulted in serious injury, including two torn ligaments. He needed surgery and missed the rest of the season to recover.

In addition to his doctors, Brady worked with body coach Alex Guerrero to speed up his recovery. A few years

Brady cradles his injured left knee in September 2008. About one month later, he had surgery to repair the knee.

earlier, Guerrero had helped eliminate pain in Brady's elbow and shoulder caused by throwing. In 2008 Brady said, "Eight weeks into my recovery [from knee surgery], I was running in the sand, and six months later—not twelve months—the discomfort in my knee was gone."

TB12 Method

Brady and Alex Guerrero created a specialized approach to fitness. The TB12 Method includes massage, nutrition, hydration, and physical and mental training. It was designed to keep Brady's body healthy and his mind sharp. He wanted to keep playing beyond 40, and he was willing to dedicate his diet and lifestyle to accomplishing that goal. In Brady's book, *The TB12 Method: How to Do What You Love, Better and for Longer*, he wrote, "I began to take preventative measures against being in pain, or getting hurt, rather than waiting to get hurt before I did something about it."

Brady wanted to share the TB12 Method with others. So he and Guerrero launched the TB12 Sports Therapy Center in Foxborough, Massachusetts, in 2013, and another center in Tampa, Florida, in 2020. The centers are designed to help athletes prepare their bodies and minds, sustain their fitness, and recover from injuries.

Brady and Alex Guerrero

Gisele Bündchen and Brady in 2010

Though Brady was away from football for the 2008 season, his life was eventful in other ways. He was dating Gisele Bündchen, a highly successful fashion model from Brazil. In January 2009, Brady got down on one knee to propose, and Bündchen became alarmed and asked him to get up. She was concerned that kneeling would harm his injured knee, but she accepted his proposal.

Brady and Bündchen held a private wedding ceremony at a Catholic church in Santa Monica, California, in February 2009. They invited only family and close friends. The couple also visited Horizontina, Bündchen's hometown in Brazil. In April they held a small wedding celebration on the beach in Costa Rica. Capping off an exciting year, the newlyweds welcomed their first child, a son named Benjamin, in December. Their second child, Vivian, arrived three years later in December 2012.

STUNNING VICTORY

Brady's knee healed in time to play in the 2009 season. In November he became the career leader in passing yards for the Patriots, surpassing Drew Bledsoe. It took a few more seasons for the Patriots to return to the Super Bowl. In 2012 they had a rematch with the New York Giants, and once again, the Giants won the game and took home the Lombardi Trophy. This time, the Giants won by four points, 21–17.

In 2012 Junipero Serra High School wanted to name its football stadium after Brady, who was already a member of the school's Hall of Fame. In addition to honoring his incredible football career, Serra wanted to thank him for helping to raise thousands of dollars in scholarship money for the school. Brady agreed on one condition. He asked that the stadium be called Brady Family Stadium. It was important to him that his family, especially his parents, be recognized for their contribution to his success.

The Patriots' next Super Bowl appearance was in 2015. They took on the Seattle Seahawks, the defending NFL champions. Seattle's defensive backfield was known as the Legion of Boom for its big hits and tough style. The Patriots were up against a powerful opponent, but fans had confidence in Brady and his teammates.

Going into the fourth quarter, the Patriots trailed by 10 points, 24–14. But Brady had a well-earned reputation for succeeding under pressure, and he was ready. He completed 13 of 15 passes for 124 yards and

Helping Athletes

Two years after launching the first TB12 Sports Therapy Center, Brady set up a charitable arm for the business, the TB12 Foundation. It provides scholarships to at-risk and underserved athletes to access rehabilitation programs and training for improved performance. Since it began, the foundation has provided over 10,000 health and wellness treatment sessions to a diverse group of athletes. The foundation also sponsors teams that run in the Boston and New York City marathons. The TB12 Boston Marathon team raised nearly $210,000 for the foundation in 2023.

two touchdowns. With just over two minutes remaining and the Patriots ahead by four points, the Seahawks had the ball on the edge of the end zone. Surprising almost everyone, the Seahawks passed the ball instead of trying to run it in. Patriots cornerback Malcolm Butler, a rookie, beat Seattle's receiver to the ball for an interception. It was a daring play by Butler, and it worked. Seahawks players and fans were stunned. Brady and his teammates jumped up and down on the sideline, giddy with excitement at the 28–24 victory.

The team had clinched another championship, its first in a decade. Brady recognized his team's effort during the Super Bowl trophy presentation. He said, "I wanted to thank my family and all my friends, all my teammates.

Malcolm Butler (*top right*) intercepts the ball to clinch the 2015 Super Bowl for the Patriots.

I love you guys. . . . Malcolm, what a play. I mean, for a rookie to make a play like that in a Super Bowl and win us the game, it was unbelievable."

Brady returned to the University of Michigan in 2016. He had been invited by Michigan's football coach and former NFL player Jim Harbaugh. Brady brought nine-year-old Jack with him, hoping they could share a special weekend. One of the first places they visited was the Big House, the nickname for the Michigan football team's stadium, and Brady shared a video on Facebook of his son scoring a touchdown. Brady was Michigan's honorary captain for their game against Colorado, and he delivered an inspiring pregame speech to the team in the locker room. On screens throughout the stadium, the school showed video highlights from Brady's Michigan football career to the delight of fans.

Deflategate

The NFL has strict specifications for footballs used in games, including length, weight, and air pressure. Footballs are required to have 12.5 to 13.5 pounds (5.7 to 6.1 kg) of air pressure per square inch. But during a 2015 NFC playoff game between the Patriots and the Indianapolis Colts, a Colts linebacker made an interception and noticed that the ball did not seem fully inflated. The Colts brought the issue to the attention of officials on the field, and the game balls were checked and inflated according to the rules.

The NFL launched an investigation to find out why the balls had not been properly inflated. Underinflated footballs are easier for a quarterback to grip and throw. The investigation found that Patriots employees had intentionally deflated the footballs, and they wouldn't have done so without Brady's approval. Following the investigation, NFL commissioner Roger Goodell suspended Brady for four games without pay, fined the Patriots $1 million, and took away two upcoming draft picks from the team. Fans and media members called the scandal Deflategate. Brady's competitive nature was a huge part of his career success, but this time it caused him to make poor decisions that hurt his team.

FOOTBALL LEGEND

Following the Patriots' remarkable 2017 Super Bowl victory, Brady and the team won the big game again in 2019. They defeated the Los Angeles Rams 13–3. Once again, Brady delivered in the fourth quarter. With the score tied at three points, he made a pass down the field to tight end Rob Gronkowski, who was tackled at the two-yard line. Patriots running back Sony Michel soon scored to give his team the lead and the win. Brady's sixth Super Bowl victory put him alone at the top. No other player had ever won more than five Super Bowls.

The next season, the Patriots were knocked out of the playoffs by the Tennessee Titans, but New England had an even bigger issue to contend with. Brady's contract would soon end. He was willing to sign a contract extension, but the team didn't offer one that he would accept. Brady wanted a long-term deal, but the team offered only short-term contracts. Dissatisfied, he decided to find a new team to play for. In March 2020, Brady became a free agent and was able to join any team in the league.

On March 20, Brady signed a two-year, $50 million contract to join the Tampa Bay Buccaneers. He and his family were leaving New England for Florida's west coast. He would be 43 years old when the season began, the oldest player in the league.

It was mostly a whole new ball game in Tampa Bay— new team, new coach, and new colors. But not everything changed. Buccaneers teammate Chris Godwin wore jersey number 12, and he offered it to Brady out of respect for the quarterback's accomplishments. In addition to keeping his Patriots number, Brady lured former Patriots star Rob Gronkowski out of retirement to join him in Tampa Bay. Brady's eyes were set on more wins and championships with his new team.

In 2021 Brady successfully led the Buccaneers to the Super Bowl. They overcame the Kansas City Chiefs, led by Patrick Mahomes, in a dominant 31–9 victory. It was Tampa Bay's first Super Bowl win since 2003. Brady's seven Super Bowl wins are more than any other player or team has won. He also won the Super Bowl MVP award for the fifth time, setting another record.

Brady holds the Vince Lombardi Trophy for the seventh and final time after leading Tampa Bay to the title in 2021.

Brady, Inc.

Tom Brady's business interests go well beyond sports, including a line of men's clothing. In 2021 Brady cofounded Autograph, a company that sells digital collectibles such as non-fungible tokens, or NFTs. He is also a cofounder of 199 Productions, a content-creation company that makes documentaries, feature films, and television shows. 199 Productions helped create the film *80 for Brady*, which hit theaters in February 2023. Based on a true story, the film follows four women who traveled together to the 2017 Super Bowl to see Brady play. Brady appeared in the film as himself alongside a star-studded cast. Former Patriots teammates Danny Amendola, Julian Edelman, and Rob Gronkowski also played themselves in the movie.

The next season didn't end with another Super Bowl victory for Brady and the Buccaneers, but it was remarkable in other ways. In the season's fourth week, Brady faced the Patriots in Foxborough and beat them 19–17. With that win, he joined Drew Brees, Brett Favre, and Peyton Manning as the only quarterbacks in NFL history to have beaten all 32 teams. Brady also set a record for career passing yards during that game, topping Brees and his 80,358 yards. Brady ended his career with 89,214 passing yards.

In February 2022, Brady announced his retirement from the NFL. Less than two months later, he came out of retirement and rejoined the Buccaneers. In a Twitter message, he told fans that he still had more to prove on the field, and he thanked his family for supporting him. But his family was about to go through a major upheaval. In October, Brady and his wife divorced and agreed to continue co-parenting their children.

The G.O.A.T.?

In 23 NFL seasons, Tom Brady won more big games than any other player in NFL history. But is he the greatest football player of all time? Consider some of his incredible feats.

- Brady's 251 wins in the regular season and his 35 playoff victories are both NFL records.
- He is the all-time leader in passing yards (89,214) and pass completions (7,753).
- Brady earned Super Bowl MVP five times, earned league MVP three times, and was a member of 15 Pro Bowl teams.
- His 10 Super Bowl appearances and seven Super Bowl wins are both all-time records.

Brady (*right*) interacts with the audience at a 2023 tech convention in Miami, Florida. He spoke about achieving success in sports and business.

At the end of the 2023 season, Brady announced that he was permanently retiring from playing in the NFL. He was already pursuing new opportunities off the field. He bought an ownership stake in the Las Vegas Aces, a Women's National Basketball Association team. He also signed a 10-year contract to be the lead NFL analyst on Fox Sports starting in 2024.

Fans will remember the legend of Tom Brady on the gridiron for generations to come. The records he set and the championships he won over 23 years in the NFL are too great to be forgotten. Many argue that Brady is football's G.O.A.T., the greatest of all time.

IMPORTANT DATES

1977   Thomas Edward Patrick Brady Jr. is born on August 3 in San Mateo, California.

1995   Brady graduates from Junipero Serra High School.

1999   He graduates from the University of Michigan in December with a degree in general studies.

2000   Brady is drafted by the New England Patriots in the sixth round with the 199th overall pick.

2002   He wins his first NFL championship at the age of 24, becoming the youngest quarterback to win the Super Bowl.

2004   Brady leads the Patriots to a second Super Bowl victory, defeating the Carolina Panthers 32–29.

2005   He leads the Patriots to a Super Bowl victory for the second straight year, defeating the Philadelphia Eagles 24–21.

2007   Brady's son John "Jack" Moynahan is born in August.

        Brady passes for 50 touchdowns in the regular season, setting a new NFL record.

2009   Brady marries Gisele Bündchen in February. Their first child, Benjamin, arrives in December.

2012	Brady becomes the first quarterback to lead his team to 10 division titles.
	Bündchen and Brady's second child, Vivian, arrives in December.
2015	Brady leads the Patriots to a fourth Super Bowl victory, defeating the Seattle Seahawks 28–24.
2017	He leads the Patriots to the biggest comeback in Super Bowl history, defeating the Atlanta Falcons 34–28 in overtime.
2019	Brady wins his last championship with the Patriots. They beat the Rams 13–3.
2020	Brady leaves the Patriots after 20 seasons and joins the Tampa Bay Buccaneers.
2021	Brady leads the Buccaneers to a 31–9 Super Bowl win against the Kansas City Chiefs. At 43, he's the oldest quarterback to win the NFL championship.
2022	Brady retires and then returns to the NFL 40 days later to rejoin the Buccaneers.
	Brady and Bündchen divorce after 13 years of marriage.
2023	He retires permanently from playing in the NFL.

SOURCE NOTES

9   Mike D'Abate, "Patriots, Tom Brady 28–3 Super Bowl LI Comeback: Still Legendary," *Sports Illustrated*, February 5, 2023, https://www.si.com/nfl/patriots/news/new-england-patriots -super-bowl-li-comeback-tom-brady-james-white-julian -edelman-movie.

13   David Fischer, *Tom Brady: A Celebration of Greatness on the Gridiron* (Guilford, CT: Lyons, 2021), 15.

15   Fischer, 23.

18   Michael Rosenberg, "Tom Brady as You Forgot Him," *Sports Illustrated*, January 9, 2012, https://vault.si.com/vault/2012 /01/09/tom-brady-as-you-forgot-him.

21   Fischer, *Tom Brady*, 42.

22   Fischer, 54.

23   Daniel Schorn, "Transcript: Tom Brady, Part 2", CBS News, November 4, 2005, https://www.cbsnews.com/news/transcript -tom-brady-part-2/.

24   Seth Wickersham, "The Brady Hunch," *ESPN the Magazine*, accessed June 10, 2023, http://www.espn.com/magazine /vol4no26brady.html.

24   Staff of the *Boston Globe, Greatness:* The *Rise of Tom Brady* (Chicago: Triumph Books, 2005), 60.

26   Michael Silver, "Cool Customer," *Sports Illustrated*, April 15, 2002, https://vault.si.com/vault/2002/04/15/cool-customer-fresh -off-a-storybook-season-in-which-he-quarterbacked-the-patriots -to-a-super-bowl-victory-at-age-24-tom-brady-is-learning-to -cope-with-the-blitz-of-newfound-fame.

27 Silver.

29 Judy Battista, "Giants Stun Patriots in Super Bowl XLII," *New York Times*, February 4, 2008, https://www.nytimes.com /2008/02/04/sports/football/04game.html.

30 Tom Brady, *The TB12 Method: How to Do What You Love, Better and for Longer* (New York: Simon & Schuster, 2020), 25.

31 Brady, 22.

34–35 "Super Bowl 49 Patriots Trophy Presentation," YouTube video, 6:30, posted byNOSAJ, March 4, 2015 https://www.youtube.com/ watch?v=85Rgimj_moM&t=435s.

SELECTED BIBLIOGRAPHY

Battista, Judy. "Giants Stun Patriots in Super Bowl XLII." *New York Times*, February 4, 2008. https://www.nytimes.com/2008/02/04 /sports/football/04game.html.

Brady, Tom. *The TB12 Method: How to Achieve a Lifetime of Sustained Peak Performance*. New York: Simon & Schuster, 2017.

Edholm, Eric. "Tom Brady's Best Season? It Might've Been 2007, When NFL Passing Changed Forever." Yahoo Sports, February 1, 2023. https://sports.yahoo.com/tom-bradys-best-season-it-mightve-been -2007-when-nfl-passing-changed-forever-155607580.html.

Fischer, David. *Tom Brady: A Celebration of Greatness on the Gridiron*. Guilford, CT: Lyons, 2021.

Golden, Andrew, and Matt Bonesteel. "From a California Kid to the GOAT: Tom Brady through the Years." *Washington Post*, February 1, 2023. https://www.washingtonpost.com/sports/interactive/2022/tom -brady-career/.

Rosenberg, Michael. "Tom Brady as You Forgot Him." *Sports Illustrated*, January 9, 2012. https://vault.si.com/vault/2012/01/09/tom-brady-as -you-forgot-him.

Smith, Joe. "The Last Time Tom Brady Chose His Destination, He Was 18: 'It Created a Monster.'" Athletic, April 8, 2020. https://theathletic. com/1718018/2020/04/08/the-last-time-tom-brady-chose -his-destination-he-was-18-it-created-a-monster/.

Staff of the *Boston Globe*. *Greatness: The Rise of Tom Brady*. Chicago: Triumph Books, 2005.

Van Valkenburg, Kevin. "Tom Brady Felt the Michigan Love, Maybe for the First Time." *ESPN*, September 21, 2016. https://www.espn.com /nfl/story/_/id/17598609/how-deflategate-brought-tom-brady-new -england-patriots-back-university-michigan-wolverines.

Wickersham, Seth. "The Brady Hunch." *ESPN the Magazine*, accessed June 10, 2023. http://www.espn.com/magazine/vol4no26brady.html.

FURTHER READING

ESPN—Tom Brady
https://www.espn.com/nfl/player/_/id/2330/tom-brady

Lowe, Alexander. *G.O.A.T. Football Quarterbacks.* Minneapolis: Lerner Publications, 2023.

NFL—Tom Brady
https://www.nfl.com/players/tom-brady/

Pro Football Reference
https://www.pro-football-reference.com/players

Stabler, David. *Tom Brady vs. Joe Montana: Who Would Win?* Minneapolis: Lerner Publications, 2024.

Wilner, Barry. *Tom Brady and the New England Patriots.* Minneapolis: SportsZone, 2019.

INDEX

PHOTO ACKNOWLEDGMENTS

Image credits: ZUMA/Alamy, p. 2; Kevin C. Cox/Getty Images Sport/Getty Images, pp. 6, 8; Focus On Sport/Getty Images Sport/Getty Images, p. 10; AP Photo/Arthur Anderson, p. 11; Stephen Lovekin/WireImage/Getty Images, p. 12; Jallen8307/Wikimedia Commons (CC BY-SA 4.0), p. 14; Bernstein Associates/Getty Images Sport/Getty Images, p. 16; AP Photo/Duane Burleson, p. 17; Vincent Laforet/Getty Images Sport/Getty Images, p. 18; AP Photo/Paul Warner, p. 19; AP Photo/Daniel Mears, p. 20; MediaNews Group/Boston Herald/Getty Images, pp. 22, 35; Boston Globe/Getty Images, pp. 23, 30; AP Photo/Allen Kee, p. 25; Bill Frakes/Sports Illustrated/Getty Images, p. 26; John W. McDonough/ Sports Illustrated/Getty Images, p. 27; Djamilla Rosa Cochran/WireImage/Getty Images, p. 28; Kevin Mazur/Getty Images Entertainment/Getty Images, p. 31; Patrick McMullan/Getty Images, p. 32; Mike Ehrmann/Getty Images Sport/Getty Images, p. 38; Johnny Louis/Getty Images Entertainment/Getty Images, p. 41.

Cover: Gilbert Flores/Variety/Getty Images.